A–Z

OF

KNUTSFORD

PLACES - PEOPLE - HISTORY

Jean & John Bradburn

AMBERLEY

First published 2021

Amberley Publishing
The Hill, Stroud, Gloucestershire, GL5 4EP
www.amberley-books.com

Copyright © Jean & John Bradburn, 2021

The right of Jean & John Bradburn to be
identified as the Authors of this work has been
asserted in accordance with the Copyrights,
Designs and Patents Act 1988.

ISBN 978 1 4456 9678 2 (print)
ISBN 978 1 4456 9679 9 (ebook)

British Library Cataloguing in Publication Data.
A catalogue record for this book is available
from the British Library.

Typesetting by SJmagic DESIGN SERVICES,
India. Printed in Great Britain.

Contents

Introduction   4

An Accidental MP   5

Brook House   8
Baronian   9
Bucklow Hundred   10

Caldwell's Nursery   12
Cranford   13
Cross Town   14

Darkness Lane   17
Drury Lane   18

Egertons   21

Freeholders   22

Gaskell   24

(St) Helena   26
Holland Family   28
Highwaymen   30

Italianate Knutsford   32

Jacobites   36

King Street (The Bottom Street)   37

Leicester Family   44
Literature Festival   45

Mallory   47
May Day   49

Norbury Booths Hall   52
Nuclear Knutsford   53

Obelisk   54

Paratroopers   55
Penny-farthing   57
Penny   58
Princess Street (The Top Street)   59

Quarter Sessions   64

Racecourse   66
Royce, Henry   68

Silk   70
Smith, William   71
Stringer Family   72

Tatton   74
Toft Hall   76

Unitarian Chapel, Brook Street   79
Uttley   80

Vikings   83
Volunteers   84
(St) Vincent's   85

Watson's   86
Wives and Daughters   87

Xmas   88

Yankee Knutsford   91

Zeitgeist – The Spirit or Essence of a
   Particular Time   94

Acknowledgments   96
Bibliography   96
About the Authors   96

Introduction

A small town in rural Cheshire, Knutsford is full of history and fascinating architecture. Pevsner described it as 'the most attractive town of its size in Cheshire'. Legend has it that the town name was derived by King Cnut fording the river here. This is doubtful, however, as the River Lily is really no more than a brook. There is no firm evidence he came through Knutsford either, but he certainly came through Cheshire.

The two streets King Street and Princess Street are known locally as the Bottom and Top Street. Knutsford gained its market charter in 1292. The Egertons, lords of the manor, ensured the town's prosperity despite having failed in its silk and textile industry due to the lack of a canal to transport the goods.

The town has a secure place in literary history. Knutsford was the inspiration and setting for Elizabeth Gaskell's *Cranford* where she describes its characters with gentle humour and affection. She lived in Knutsford for many years and is buried in the churchyard of Brook Street Unitarian Chapel.

The town is surrounded by stately homes built by the landed gentry. It was home to Mr Royce of Rolls-Royce fame, and was home to US General Patton in the Second World War and the film of his life *Lust for Glory* included some scenes in the town. As you walk the streets you can see Italianate buildings. The town is renowned for its farmers' market and array of restaurants, bars and fine food purveyors.

A

An Accidental MP

Since 1885 Knutsford had consistently elected a Conservative MP – unsurprisingly, he was an Egerton. The one exception was in 1906 when a Liberal was elected. Things were about to change in 1997 when Martin Bell, the veteran BBC war correspondent, shocked the political world by announcing he would stand against Conservative MP Neil Hamilton in the forthcoming general election. He initially put himself forward as a candidate in Tatton, in the hope that it would spur the local Conservative organisation to deselect Neil Hamilton. This did not happen, however, and he became an MP by accident. He made the Longview Hotel his headquarters, although he was often found in a corner of the White Bear.

He appeared for his press conference on Knutsford Heath in a white suit, chosen to symbolise integrity and honour, and was thereafter dubbed 'the Man in the White Suit' by the media.

Martin Bell.

Left: The Longview Hotel.

Below: The White Bear.

Bell was surprised on Knutsford Heath by Hamilton and his wife Christine, and the opponents held a polite, if edgy, discussion in front of the gathered media. This became known as 'the Battle of Knutsford Heath'.

At almost 16,000 votes, the Conservative majority in Tatton had been their fourth largest prior to the 1997 election. The swing from that to Bell's 11,000 majority was a remarkable 48 per cent.

Though an independent, Bell most often voted with Tony Blair's Labour government in Parliament; however, on some issues – notably the banning of fox hunting and the lowering of the age of consent for homosexuals – he sided with the Conservatives.

Having promised to serve only one term as MP, Bell did not stand again in Tatton in 2001, though when polled, 82 per cent of his constituents said they wished that he would. He later said he regretted making the promise. Bell stood as an independent candidate for the UK's eastern region in the June 2004 elections to the European Parliament, but was unsuccessful, winning only 6.2 per cent of the vote. He retired from politics after this.

On 3 July 1997, a parliamentary enquiry found Hamilton guilty of taking cash for questions. He brought a libel action against Mohamed Al-Fayed, which he lost and was declared bankrupt. Martin was warmly welcomed to the literature festival in 2000, the year his book *An Accidental MP* was published.

An Accidental MP.

Brook House

This was the home of Lady Jane Stanley. She was the daughter of the 11th Earl of Derby and she became Knutsford's first aristocratic resident when she moved there in 1780.

The house stood at the bottom of Adams Hill in Brook Street, close to the Unitarian Chapel. The fine house is long gone but it had lovely gardens and stables, and the River Lily ran through the grounds.

Lady Jane was in her fifties when she moved to the town so she could visit her many aristocratic relatives around the county. She never married, and this possibly led to certain bitterness.

> A maid I lived a maid I died
> I never was asked and never denied.

She was a well-known character around the town. She would walk the narrow streets and expected men to give way to her. If they did not they may well be hit by her cane.

Brook House.

She knew her own worth and did not hesitate to dictate her views to the people of Knutsford. She paid to have pavements laid along the street, but again she demanded that they be narrow and not wide enough for man and women to walk side by side.

She was horrified when her brother Edward Smith-Stanley, 12th Earl of Derby, married an actress – Elizabeth Farren. Lady Jane was wealthy enough to have a sedan chair and it would be a familiar sight to see her being carried around the town. This chair can still be seen in the Knutsford May Day procession. She is thought to be the model for Mrs Gaskell's Lady Ludlow. Her name of course lives on in Stanley Road which was originally Love Lane.

Baronian

Zarch and Shushan Baronian had five sons and a daughter, and they lived at Brae Cottage in Legh Road. Zarch was a merchant who exported to China. The family were originally from Turkey and they tragically lost their son Haron in the First World War.

Haron was born in Manchester in 1896 and the family later moved to Knutsford. He was educated at Bowdon College and then went on to study at Manchester University. When war broke out in 1914, and finding he could not obtain a commission, he enlisted as a private in the Cheshire Regiment. He served with the Expeditionary Force in Mesopotamia and was wounded on 1 February 1917 and admitted to hospital at Basra. He rejoined his regiment upon recovery but was killed in action on 11 April. His friend Arthur King wrote:

> On 10 April we received the news that the Turks, in large force, were attempting to outflank us. We had breakfast together and this was the last time I saw Haron alive. The next time I saw him, poor Haron, was lying just as if he had gone to sleep His eyes were closed, and there was no sign of his being hit. Only a tell-tale little bullet hole in his tunic showed where he had been shot through the stomach.

The family commissioned a statue to commemorate their beloved son and other sons of Knutsford. The statue is bronze, showing Haron in field dress and was designed by Hamo Thorneycroft. It stood in the gardens of the family home, Brae Cottage, on Legh Road. In the 1970s the statue was installed in front of the War Memorial Cottage Hospital.

This fine statue is now in pride of place in the centenary garden in front of the library.

In his welcome to guests Councillor Coan said, 'The town council had decided the town deserved a fitting memorial to its fallen, one that was central, protected and accessible to all. The statue was commissioned by his family, and it is with the family's blessing that the statue now finally becomes part of the town's Centennial War Memorial.' The memorial also lists the many other brave men of Knutsford who died for their country.

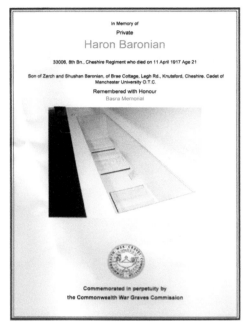

Above left: An 'In Memory' certificate for Haron Baronian from the Commonwealth War Graves website.

Above right: Baronian statue in the centenary garden, Toft Road.

Bucklow Hundred

In early times Cheshire was divided into hundreds for law and local government. The hundred of Bucklow spread as far north as Sale and west to Runcorn. The court was held at Bucklow Hill, which is now just a hamlet outside the town. The area was later governed by the Bucklow Rural District Council, who oversaw a large area including Toft, Bexton and Ollerton from 1897 to 1974. The headquarters can still be seen on the corner of Bexton Road and Stanley Road. It is an outstanding building with superb terracotta and quality brickwork.

An important responsibility for these councils was the provision for the poor. Knutsford's workhouse was spread over a large area of Bexton Road, on the site of the Community Hospital. The 1834 Poor Law Amendment Act established nine Poor Law unions in Cheshire, each with its own workhouse. Workhouses were supposed to be a deterrent to the able-bodied pauper. Under the Act, poor relief would only be granted to those who passed the 'workhouse test'; in other words, you would have to be desperate to enter a workhouse.

The elderly, infirm, orphans, mentally ill and single mothers were all accommodated, but life inside the workhouse was intended to be as off-putting as possible. Men,

Former Bucklow
Rural District Council
offices, on the corner
of Stanley Road.

women, children, the infirm and the able-bodied were all housed separately. Food was basic and monotonous – gruel, a watery porridge or bread and cheese. Inmates had to wear the rough workhouse uniform and sleep in dormitories. Baths were allowed – supervised – once a week.

The able-bodied were given hard work such as stone breaking or picking apart old ropes. Families were only allowed minimal access to one another, and in the early days were not even allowed to speak to each other outside these access times. The workhouse came to be seen as the ultimate degradation.

Some people only stayed in the workhouse briefly and when there was no other option; others spent their entire lives in the same workhouse. As medical care was expensive, the poorest women would sometimes come to the workhouse hospital to give birth. The Victorian workhouse was a dreaded institution, but it did provide the only source of medical treatment for the poor before the NHS.

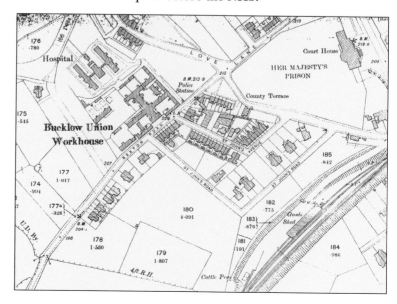

Map of Bucklow
workhouse, 1910.

Caldwell's Nursery

This was a very famous local business with six generations on Chelford Road. Caldwell's reputation for selling quality trees and plants was renowned, and they supplied trees and plants countrywide. Their client list included all the local stately homes: Tatton Hall, Booths Hall, Birtles Hall and Quarry Bank Mill.

It was in 1780 when the first William Caldwell arrived in Knutsford, at the age of fourteen, and was apprenticed to John Nickson. William's father was a nurseryman at Knowsley in Lancashire and also had a business in Liverpool for the sale of flour. The nursery was originally named Nickson & Carr but it later became Caldwell's. The business prospered and by the late 1840s the nurseries of William Caldwell occupied over 27 acres in Nether Knutsford.

The Caldwell family in 1908. William Caldwell is seated alongside his sister Hada who worked at the nurseries. Standing are his son Billie and, from the left, his daughters Winnie, Lucy, Madge and Maud. (Courtesy of David Caldwell)

Caldwell's, Chelford Road, 1870.

As well as the main site on Chelford Road, he also owned nursery grounds in Nether Knutsford at Shaw Heath and at Ollerton. It was a sad for the town when the company closed in January 1992. The flower shop passed from Caldwell's to the shop manager, Jack Daniels, in 1966 and he operated the business until his death in 1976.

Cranford

This delightful story of life in Knutsford was first published as a serial in *Household Words* at the end of 1851. The book has assured the town a place in literary history. It is still Mrs Gaskell's most well-known book and has never been out of print. It could only have been written by a woman who had spent her happy childhood in this funny little town observing the eccentric characters. The strict social etiquette would have been well observed by Mrs Gaskell. The novel is a series of vignettes in the life of the genteel ladies of *Cranford*. She tells their story with ironic humour and affection, although her opening sentence perhaps tells a different story: '*Cranford* is in possession of the Amazons; all the holders of houses, above a certain rent, are women. If a married couple come to settle in the town, somehow the gentleman disappears.'

They lived in elegant economy but observed strict social etiquette. The main character is Miss Matty Jenkins, although all of her characters are described with

An illustration from the 1898 edition of *Cranford* showing Miss Matty's fear of the sedan chair.

kindness and sympathy for their human foibles. Miss Matty stands out as full of gentleness and a complete lack of affectation. She never married. There was sadness but no bitterness, and she was keen for Martha (her servant) to have a follower and find happiness. Many of the events described actually happened in the town: the bank really did fail; the cow really did fall into the lime pit; and the magician, Signor Brunoni, really did perform at the assembly room in the Royal George.

Cross Town

Cross Town was always a distinct community from Knutsford, across the moor. There was an actual cross there, described by Sir Peter Leicester as standing at the top of the hill (Hollow Lane) on the way to Mobberley. It was a poor community. The weavers' cottages by The Builders Arms housed pieceworkers and most of the men were farm labourers. This was often a source of tension with Knutsford.

There was a church built in 1858, but it was unsafe and demolished in 1879. When the Legh family sold land in Cross Town the area was altered, becoming home to wealthier families who built grand houses. Thorneyholme was built in around 1880 by Charles Galloway.

We can see him in the 1891 census living here with his wife Annie, two sons, a daughter, a cook and two housemaids. He had made his money making ships' boilers. Nearby was Woodlands, the home of Henry Long Tanner, and others such as Aylesby and Rockford Lodge. Only Sharston House still remains.

Right: The Lodge to Thornyholme.

Below: Cross Town, 1872.

Woodlands became Woodside Day and Boarding School for Boys before demolition. Thorneyholme was requisitioned in the war and later bought by Cheshire County Council, who sadly demolished the house and built Manor Park housing estate. The lodge still stands, opposite Manor Park School.

Cross Town became a parish in 1858. Its new wealth enabled a new, grander church to be built with donations from the richer families. The new church was designed by Paley and Austin in 1880. The tower was added later and the spire of the original design was never built. Saint Cross dominates the view from across the moor. Across the road was Cross Town School, which has now been demolished. The community even had its own silver band, which amalgamated with Knutsford's band in 1889. May Day also caused problems as the locals believed that the May Queen was never chosen from Cross Town. There was further ill feeling when the route of the procession eliminated Cross Town. They decided to have their own festival from 1876; it lasted four years.

The view across the moor to Cross Town.

D

Darkness Lane

Darkness Lane, as described by Mrs Gaskell, was believed to be haunted by a headless lady and infested with robbers and was in fact Brook Street, leading to Chelford Road. 'Miss Matty having braved the dangers of Darkness Lane and thus a stack of reputation of braveness to fall back on.'

At the corner of this street was the oldest cottage in Knutsford. The corner was known as 'Stormy Point'. Long gone now is the Congregational church that stood on the right. The foundation stone was laid in 1865 and Sir James Watt of Cheadle had paid for the fine building, which was constructed in a Gothic Revival style. The spire was magnificent too, but unfortunately subsidence caused the church to be demolished in 1948.

Caldwell's nursery was on the left. Further up, in Chelford Road, Over Knutsford, are the pump cottages and the Dame School. Joan Leach tells us that the school mistress was barely literate.

Brook Street, described as 'Darkness Lane' in *Cranford*.

The Dame School.

Drury Lane

Of all the interesting streets in Knutsford, Drury Lane must be the most unique. Starting at the bottom, you have the site of Richard Watt's steam laundry. It was built in 1898 on the site of a tannery and is quite a unique building with its tower, green tiles and minarets. The plan was to provide work and housing for the people and the houses were built in the same Mediterranean style, with long, narrow windows and verandas.

Drury Lane, looking down to the laundry.

At the top of Drury Lane we have the wonderful Ruskin Rooms. Watt was a great admirer of John Ruskin and named the building after him. Built in 1902, the Ruskin Rooms provided a social club for the laundry workers. It was also used as a club for American soldiers during the Second World War.

Drury Lane.

Ruskin Rooms, Drury Lane.

Above: Ruskin Rooms. (Courtesy of Tony Grist)

Left: Patton's plaque on the Ruskin Rooms.

E

Egertons

The Egertons were an ancient Cheshire family that resided at Oulton Park, near Tarporley, since the Middle Ages. The family owned much of Cheshire and the name lives on in pubs all over the county.

The Tatton branch of the Egerton family descended from the female line from Thomas Egerton of Tatton Park in Cheshire, the youngest son of John Egerton, 2nd Earl of Bridgewater. His grandaughter Hester (d. 1780) married William Tatton and in 1780 they assumed, by royal licence, the surname of Egerton in lieu of Tatton. Samuel Egerton was guardian to the young Duke of Bridgewater and was supportive in ensuring his famous canal was built.

The last Lord Egerton, Maurice, never married and on his death in 1958 the title was extinct and the park was given to the National Trust. This ended 350 years of Egertons as lords of the manor of Knutsford. He was a shy and solitary figure who spent most of his time not in Cheshire but on his estate in Kenya, where he enjoyed big-game hunting.

He was a supporter of local youth – but only of boys. He founded the Egerton Boys' Club on Mere Heath Lane to encourage the Knutsford youngsters to play sport and be involved in health-giving physical activity in the great outdoors. He banned girls and was known as a misogynist. He was often seen in town looking like an ordinary workman in his cloth cap.

Freeholders

The Knutsford freeholders guarded the town's ancient right to common land. We owe them gratitude for protecting our beloved heath from development. They were, of course, wealthy landowners themselves and included the Egertons, the Leghs of Booths, the Hollands and the Caldwells. They also played a part in providing services to the town. They paid £150 in 1854 to provide five handsome classical gaslights; however, it took forty years for them to actually be lit. The last one remains on the corner of Mere Heath Lane.

In 1888, the freeholders railed the heath to prevent gypsies taking it over. Lord Egerton was angry as he was not consulted, but he agreed reluctantly when gateways were added to allow some access.

It was the freeholders who laid out Ladies Mile, trying to prevent it becoming an out of the way haunt of prostitutes.

Freeholders lamp corner, Toft Road.

F

When Maurice Egerton died much of the land in Knutsford was sold to the Brooks family of Peover Hall. In 1973, the issue of the common land of the heath was fought in court – Randle Brooks vs the freeholders. There was proof that sales of common land included parts of the heath. It was sadly decided that the freeholders' right to common land had lapsed and it was ruled that the Brooks family had official title to the land. Thankfully, a Commons bill in 2006 gave added protection to common land, although the controversy remains.

Although it is now established that Tatton Estate own the heath, when they proposed the Pub in the Park festival there was local opposition. Friends of The Heath Society opposed the plan because it would have interfered with public access and deprived local people of the use of part of the heath for ten days and involved enclosure, which could have been unlawful. The Pub in The Park switched to The Lambing Shed last year following opposition to the staging of the event on the heath. Tatton Estate say:

> Events like the Royal May Day, the circus, and Scouts car boot sale – joined last year by the very successful Knutsford Lions charity event – have been conducted on the heath for as long as anyone can remember. The heath will always remain a jewel in Knutsford's crown in the Tatton Estate's careful stewardship.

Gaskell

Mrs Gaskell has put Knutsford on the international map. The Gaskell Society, founded by Joan Leach in 1985, welcomes members from all over the world. Gaskell was born Elizabeth Cleghorn Stevenson in Lindsey Row, now Cheyne Walk, Chelsea, in September 1810. Her father was William Stevenson, a Scotsman and a Unitarian minister. He later became keeper to the Treasury of London, but he also wrote articles – perhaps this is where she inherited her talent for writing? His obituary said, 'The literary and scientific world has sustained a great loss in the death of William Stevenson, a man remarkable for his stores of knowledge.' His earliest post was as a classical tutor in the Manchester Academy, so there was always a northern connection. Her mother was a daughter of the Holland family of Sandlebridge, near Knutsford. Gaskell was only a month old when she tragically lost her mother, and she was sent to Knutsford in the care of her aunt, Hannah Lumb. This was a happy time and she spent her childhood living at Heathwaite, overlooking the heath.

Mrs Gaskell.

Heathwaite, Mrs Gaskell's childhood home overlooking the heath.

She referred to Knutsford as her 'dear adopted town'. 'The houses are anything but regular they may be mean in detail but all together they look very well.' She went to school in Stratford on Avon, but on returning to Knutsford she met and married Revd William Gaskell, a Unitarian minister at Cross Street Chapel. They married in 1832 at Knutsford Parish Church, as was the law at this time for Unitarians. She then made her home in Manchester and dedicated her life to works of charity. In 1850, they moved to Plymouth Grove and she wrote, 'We have got a house. Yes we really have. And if I had neither conscience or prudence I would be delighted as it certainly is a beauty.' The house has been lovingly restored and can be visited today.

The couple had four daughters, but tragically their son Willie died of scarlet fever. This led William to encourage her to take up writing and her experiences of poverty and disease in Manchester influenced her first book *Mary Barton*. After the success of this book she made many friends in the literary world, including Charles Dickens and the Brontë sisters. She even received a letter of congratulation from Thomas Carlyle, who had lived nearby to her father's home in Chelsea. She went on to write a number of books, and Knutsford featured in many of them. In 1857 she wrote a biography of her beloved friend Charlotte Brontë. She wrote the truth as she saw it, but the family challenged some of her work. The first edition was withdrawn and she found the whole episode very distressing. After revision, the second edition went on to become very successful. She purchased a house in Hampshire with the income from her books. She was staying here with her daughters and writing her last novel, *Wives and Daughters*, when she died suddenly of heart disease, aged fifty-five. The family brought her back to Knutsford and she is buried in the graveyard at Brook Street Chapel.

(St) Helena

St Helena, the mother of Constantine I, is believed to have discovered the cross upon which Jesus Christ was crucified. It is a mystery why St Helena's Chapel was dedicated to her. This ancient chapel sat in countryside near Longridge. If you stroll through St John's Wood and then turn right for Longridge you will come upon this sacred place, which was once Knutsford's parish church. It was built by the Legh family on land north-east of the Norbury Booths. Sir John Legh was buried here in 1660. The chapel was used by the family and their tenants even after St John's Church was built in Knutsford. The bells of the old chapel were recast and mounted in the new church. The last burial was in 1802 and the tower was finally toppled by a gale in 1877. Until quite recently, Sunday school children from Knutsford would make an annual pilgrimage to the deserted chapel. Sadly, the stones are now well weathered, and it is hard to read the inscriptions.

All that remains of St Helena's Chapel.

St John's Church.

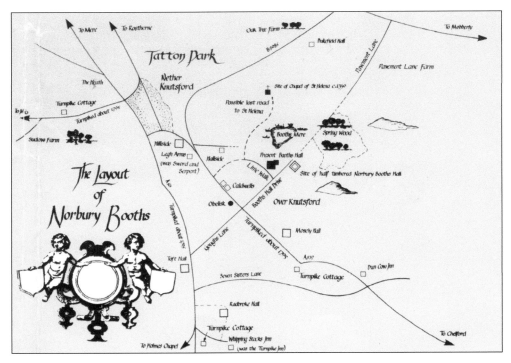

Map of Norbury Booths showing the site of the ancient chapel.

Holland Family

Mrs Gaskell was related to the Holland family, a prominent family who held estates in Sandlebridge and Great Warford. Her mother was Peter Holland's sister, Elizabeth, who married William Stevenson. It was another sister, Hannah Lumb, who brought Elizabeth up. Peter, a doctor, was believed to be the model for Mr Gibson – the country doctor in *Wives and Daughters*. He developed a large eminent practice around Knutsford and attended all the leading families: the Leicesters of Tabley, the Egertons at Tatton, the Stanleys of Alderley and the Greggs at Quarry Bank Mill in Styal.

Peter Hill lived at Church House, right next to St John's. Elizabeth spent many happy hours with his daughters Mary and Lucy. This beautiful house was built around 1760. The property had extensive gardens that stretched down to King Street and towards the station on Toft Road. It is now named Hollingford House and his home to Arthur Lee.

Peter's son Henry was also a successful physician in London. His son – also Henry – became 1st Lord Knutsford, although he did say he considered 'Lord Cranford' as his title. The Knutsford coat of arms contains the motto of the Holland family: *'Respice, aspice, prospice'*, meaning look to the past, the present and the future.

Right: Plaque on Hollingford House, Toft Road.

Below: Hollingford House.

Knutsford coat of arms.

Highwaymen

Knutsford can boast two famous highwaymen. Dick Turpin was suspected of committing a robbery near Dunham Downs. He then commanded his horse, Black Bess, to ride at breakneck speed to The Kilton Inn at Hoo Green. He approached the groom and demanded to know the time, thus establishing an alibi, as it was not believed he could have got to The Kilton from Dunham in such a short time. He was believed. He eventually met his end in York where he was executed in 1739 for horse theft.

The second notorious highwayman actually lived in Knutsford. Edward Higgins came to Knutsford in 1757 when he married a local girl named Katherine Birtles. They were married at the parish church and he was described as a 'gentleman' in the parish register. They made their home in an elegant house overlooking the heath, very close to Mrs Gaskell's childhood home. The house was at this time covered in ivy and known as the 'Cann Office', on account of it having once been the place in which scales and weights were tested.

Wives were not expected to be unduly inquisitive about their husband's business affairs, and Katherine was probably satisfied to be told that Edward owned property in various parts of the country and lived on the rents.

In 1754, Edward was convicted of a breaking into a house at Worcester and sentenced to transportation for seven years. But the American colonies could not hold our Edward for long. Shortly after arrival in Boston he stole a large amount of money from the house of a rich merchant and bought himself a passage home. He was back in England a few months after being transported. For a while he lived

Heath House, the home of Highwayman Higgins.

in Manchester, before realising the many grand homes around Knutsford would provide rich pickings.

Higgins and his wife dined with their neighbours and he hunted, fished and shot with them. Such a life enabled him to become familiar with the layout of his hosts' houses, and so he was able to sneak back for a spot of burglary later.

Once, when dining with the Egertons of Oulton Park, he took a fancy to a jewelled snuff box lying on the table. During the night he stole the box and then hid it outdoors for later recovery. The next morning when the theft was discovered, he earned much approval by summoning all the servants together and having their rooms searched! Needless to say, it was not found there.

Besides burgling the homes of his friends in Knutsford, Higgins also went out some nights, muffling the hooves of his horse so as not to disturb the neighbours (he was a considerate person) and held up a coach or two on the Chester Road. One evening he spotted Lady Warburton in the Assembly Rooms wearing exquisite diamonds and he decided he would have them. He left early and took the road to Arley. He saw the family coach approaching, but to his dismay she saw him and hailed him, which put paid to his plan.

A silver race cup disappeared from The George Inn. Also, when Samuel Egerton of Tatton reported money stolen from his desk Higgins came under suspicion. The constables came to his home, but he managed to evade them and afterwards there was a suspicion that there was a secret tunnel over to the heath.

Higgins moved to Bristol, but his luck ran out when he was caught breaking into a house in Carmarthen. Once identified as an escaped prisoner, his fate was sealed. After being sentenced to death he wrote, 'I beg you will have compassion on my poor disconsolate widow and fatherless infants, as undoubtedly you will hear my widow upbraided with my past misconduct. I beg you will vindicate her as not being guilty of knowing about my villainy.'

Italianate Knutsford

Richard Harding Watt, a wealthy glove merchant from Manchester, came to Knutsford in 1895. He was not an architect, but his building designs were inspired by his travels around the Mediterranean and in particular his love of Italy.

His house on Legh Road, The Croft, was built for him by Bowden architect John Brooke. In 1907, William Longworth added a tower to The Croft. The house has two storeys, the lower storey being in brick and the upper storey and tower in roughcast brick with a plain tiled roof.

The Croft, home of Richard Harding Watt.

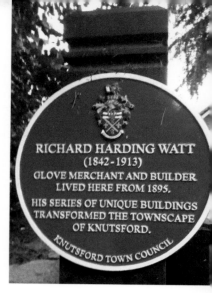

Plaque in memory of Richard Harding Watt.

He then went on to design further striking unique buildings along Legh Road, most of which were built in rendered brick and with pantile roof:

White Howe, 1901

This is a two-storey house designed by Walter Aston in roughcast brick with a pantiled hip roof. It has two towers of differing sizes.

Lake House, 1902

A three-storey house, constructed in rendered brick with stone dressings and a pantile roof. At the east end is a round tower with an irregular parapet. It also contains an oriel window.

Breeze, 1902

This originated as stable and a gardener's flat for Lake House and was only later converted into a house. It was designed by Walter Aston. It is in two storeys and has a three-storey tower surmounted by a cupola.

High Morland, 1903

Again, designed by William Longworth in rendered brick with stone dressings, it has three storeys. Linked to the house by a lower bay is a tower with an overhanging pyramidal roof. The Lodge has a tower at the rear.

Above: High Morland.

Left: The Lodge.

Woodgarth, 1904

This is a two-storey house with an L-plan designed by Percy Worthington. Unusually, it is in roughcast brick with stone dressings and has a plain tiled roof. The interior includes Arts and Crafts features.

Broad Terraces, 1905

This is constructed in rendered brick with a pyramidal pantile roof. It has a square belvedere tower, also with a pyramidal roof. There are Italianate and classical architectural features, including Doric columns.

Aldwarden Hill.

Aldwarden Hill, 1906

This is again constructed in rendered brick with ashlar dressings, random projecting blocks and a pantile roof. The house is in two storeys, surmounted by a belvedere.

Chantry Dane, 1906

Constructed in rendered brick with stone dressings and pantile roofs. It is in three storeys and its features include an Ionic porch at the front, a tower and a bellcote.

These houses stood on a marshy hill known as Sanctuary Moor. They also overlooked Paradise Garage on Toft Road, which was described by Henry Green as an eden for aquatic animals. This is the reason for the name Toft Road Paradise Garage. Pevsner dubbed Legh Road 'the maddest sequence of villas in all England'. He then went on to enhance the town with a further unique building, Gaskell Memorial Tower and King's Coffee House.

In March 1913, he was travelling to the railway station from his home. He often stood in the carriage to admire the views, but on this occasion he fell from his carriage and died of his injuries.

Jacobites

In 1714, when Queen Anne died, George I became king, but James Francis Edward Stuart ('the Old Pretender') was still hoping to take what he believed was his rightful crown. He was the son of James II and VII of England, Scotland and Ireland. Catholics had been excluded from the English crown, ensuring that a Protestant became king.

The Catholic Stuart family had many supporters in the county. A group of Cheshire gentry met at Ashley Hall to decide whether to support the Catholic cause: Henry and Peter Legh, John Warren, Robert Cholmondeley and Sir Richard Grosvenor. It was a split vote, but the chairman Thomas Assheton decided discretion was the better part of valour and not to support the Stuart cause. There was fear of trouble and the militia was called out to Knutsford Heath in October 1715. Orders were sent out by Samul Daniel of Over Tabley Hall for mustering. Every soldier was to appear armed with a musket, powder and bullets. Edward Stanley of Alderley declared this not possible at such short notice and in November they assembled on the heath and marched to Manchester.

The Jacobites surrendered at Preston. James Francis Edward Stuart returned to France, sailing from Montrose on 5 February 1716. The abandonment of his rebel allies caused ill-feeling against him in Scotland and he found himself unwelcome in France. The Cheshire gentry made a wise decision to celebrate: they had their portraits taken, and these can still be seen around the staircase at Tatton Hall. Following James's failure, attention turned to his son 'Bonny' Prince Charlie, who led a doomed uprising in 1745. With the failure of this second rebellion, the Stuart hopes of regaining the British throne were effectively destroyed.

King Street (The Bottom Street)

This is the oldest and most attractive street in the town, and many of the buildings were built in the sixteenth century or even earlier. Most of the buildings are listed buildings.

The arrival of the railway transformed the corner at the bottom of Adam's Hill and King Street forever. Henry Green had described Adam's Hill as a 'wild dell'. Cottages were demolished to make way for the railway bridge. The railway had been opposed by many locals, but there is no doubt it changed Knutsford. Many rich merchants would make the town their home and now access to Manchester was easier. The station opened on 12 May 1862. As you pass along Bottom Street many fine cottages remain. The stocks stood under the church wall.

St John's Church was designed in neoclassical style by J. Garlive. It is constructed in brick with stone dressings and has a slate roof. In 1879, the chancel was extended and

King Street, looking down to the railway bridge.

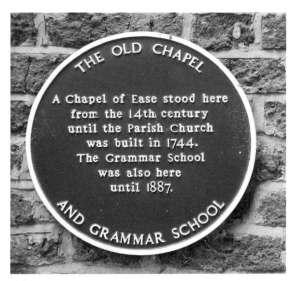

THE OLD CHAPEL

A Chapel of Ease stood here
from the 14th century
until the Parish Church
was built in 1744.
The Grammar School
was also here
until 1887.

AND GRAMMAR SCHOOL

Plaque on King Street, opposite
St John's.

reordered by Alfred Darbyshire. Opposite was the original chapel of ease before the church was built. This building became the grammar school.

Next we come to Richard Watt's last enterprise. John Howard reminds us, 'circa 1850 my great great grandfather purchased an array of dilapidated buildings midway along King Street, which included shops, cottages, stables, a smithy, coach house and an inn, the Hat and Feather.' Later the brothers sold their various properties to Richard Harding Watt. Having acquired the properties, Watt promptly demolished them for his new project.

Designed by William Longworth as a memorial tower to Mrs Gaskell, a coffee house and council offices, it is constructed in rubble sandstone with Portland stone at the top of the tower. Its architectural style is eclectic Italianate with Arts and Crafts elements. There is a tower with a dome, a statue of Mrs Gaskell in a niche, a bronze medallion and a pair of large Doric columns, which were moved from St Peter's Church in Manchester. The dedication ceremony was on 25 March 1907 when Mrs Gaskell's grandson represented the family. There had been opposition from the council, which Richard admitted when he gave his speech 'I had no wish to monopolise the honour of paying homage to Mrs Gaskell whose works have given me great delight.'

His aim when planning King's Coffee House was to provide a sophisticated salon, a place for refreshment but also for intellectual conversation. In addition to providing food and drink, the coffee house was stocked with newspapers and journals. He had realised that perhaps the working men of Knutsford would not forsake the many pubs in the town. He believed if he was to attract the artists and intellectuals he would need to appoint the right managers. He engaged Alice and Ethel Wilson – both artists who had connections with liberal Manchester. Indeed, Emily Pankhurst, the suffragette leader, visited the coffee house. John Galsworthy and Lowry are also said to have visited. The building later became La Belle Epoque and is now sadly empty.

Right: Gaskell Tower.

Below left: Plaque on Gaskell Tower.

Below right: King's Coffee House.

GASKELL
MEMORIAL TOWER
Built in 1907.
Designed for Richard Harding Watt.

Dedicated to Elizabeth Gaskell
the 19th century author.

KNUTSFORD TOWN COUNCIL

King's Coffee House
lounge.

The Rose and Crown is built in a black and white, half-timbered style with slanting gable and is another well-preserved example of what Knutsford pubs used to look like. It carries the date '1041', but this should actually read 1641. The top of the six was chipped off more than fifty years ago and was never replaced.

The Royal George Hotel is steeped in history. Built in the fourteenth century, the tavern was originally called the White Swan. Its name is thought to come from the time of the Wars of the Roses, when Queen Margaret visited Chester in 1455 and distributed swan emblems to be worn as a token of love to the king. It was renamed The George and Dragon in 1727.

The 'royal' prefix was added in 1832 when the Duchess of Kent visited with the young Princess Victoria, five years before she became queen. The dragon was dropped. They stayed there as guests during visits to Chatsworth. Another somewhat more ominous patron was Highwayman Higgins (alias Edward Hickson) who lived a double life in the 1750s and 1760s, wining and dining by day and burgling the local gentry by night.

Gaskell Tower and The
Rose and Crown.

Above: Saint George and the Dragon.

Right: The Royal George.

The George used to house a desk in an alcove under the stairs in the hall. This was believed to have been used by frequent patron Lord Nelson when arranging a rendezvous with Lady Hamilton, who lived in Cheshire. Mrs Gaskell wrote many scenes set in the Royal George, such as when the ladies went to see the magical tricks of conjurer Signor Brunoni in the pub's assembly room.

The elegant assembly rooms were added in the mid-eighteenth century by the Cromwell Legh family who owned the hotel. The George's yard stretched right up to Princess Street and provided coach houses and stabling for many horses. The mail coaches would be coming and going day and night. It has always been the most prestigious of the many coaching inns in Knutsford.

The Angel was also an important coaching stop. Originally, The Angel was known as The Mermaid and stood on the opposite side of King Street. The Angel was immortalised in the pages of *Cranford*. In the novel, this pub was where Lord Mauleverer stayed when the impoverished Captain Brown's house proved too humble. The Angel is difficult to date because it has gone through many changes, but its main front is eighteenth century. It was the centre for the racecourse on the heath. 'All horses had to be entered at the inn between two and seven pm and all certification should be produced.'

Above: The Angel.

Left: Marble Arch.

In the 1950s it became the place to be seen. There was a thriving nightclub, attracting the Cheshire set and sports cars were often seen parked outside. Opposite is the pretty Marble Arch. Beyond that is the entrance to Tatton Park.

Above: Marble Arch plaque.

Below: Entrance to Tatton Park.

Leicester Family

The Leicester family owned the estate at Tabley for 700 years. John de Leicester built the moated hall in 1380. He had profited as a knight in the French wars under John of Gaunt. The family were forever feuding. His mother was Mary of Mobberley and his uncle Ralph had no sons. He therefore named his nephew John as heir. Not surprisingly his daughters and their husbands disputed this, resulting in the murder of his brother-in-law Hugh de Chadderton. John fled to Coventry after stealing family jewels and he was arrested and sent to Chester Castle. The old moated hall had been greatly altered when Sir Francis Leicester decided a hall must be built. He feared the land was unhealthy and wanted to resite the hall. John Carr of York designed the

Tabley House.

fine Palladium Hall in 1767. Tabley House boasts twin curved staircases leading up to the portico and fine craftsmanship. Sir John Fleming Leicester was a patron of the arts and spent much of the family fortune on fine art. Much of his collection can still be seen at Tabley. The family were keen on drama and loved performing in plays. Cuthbert Leicester Warren converted part of the stable block into a fully equipped 120-seat theatre in the early 1930s. The last owner was Colonel John Leicester Warren. He started a boarding school at the hall. His death, in 1975, ended 700 years of Leicesters at Tabley. Their legacy includes some of the finest art, furniture and books that money could buy, as well as a fascinating family history. Tabley House is owned by the University of Manchester. The mansion is open to the public and includes some of the artworks by great British painters such as Turner, Lawrence and Reynolds, and furniture by great British makers such as Gillow, Bullock and Chippendale. St Peter's Chapel, originally built on an island in the Mere in 1678, was moved in 1927 and re-erected on its present site adjacent to the house. The chapel has impressive stained glass, with one window designed by Burne-Jones.

Literature Festival

The Literature Festival has been the highlight of autumn in Knutsford since 2000. The festival began as a one-off event to mark the millennium. Joan Leach, Marie Moss and Audrey Young were on the first committee. There was a celebrity dinner at Cottons Hotel, and Margaret Drabble and her husband Michael Holroyd were the guest speakers. Joanna Trollope was the speaker at the literary lunch at the Royal George. Many other notable authors spoke at the festival including P. D. James, Martin Bell and Jenny Uglow. There were theatre performances, a literary walk and even a coach tour. Another innovation was a literature price to encourage young literary talent. It was

Literature lunch.

The Mere.

a huge success and following it the festival celebrated its 20th anniversary in 2019. Over the years many famous faces have visited the festival: Douglas Hurd, William Hague, Roy Hattersley, Joan Bakewell, David Starkey, Kate Adie, Michael Portillo, Pru Leith and John Suchet. In 2000, there were only a few famous festivals; now literature festivals have sprung up all over the country, but Knutsford was one of the first.

M

Mallory

This is the story of George Mallory, our very own local hero and who may well have made the first ascent to the top of Mount Everest. Everest is not only the highest mountain in the world, it was also the last of the great challenges. Mallory was born in Mobberley, the son of Herbert Leigh Mallory, the vicar of St Winifred's Church. The church has long been associated with the Mallory family. You can still see the stained-glass windows dedicated to George Mallory.

His father had owned the lovely Jacobean Mobberley Old Hall. George had two sisters and a younger brother. He was raised on Hobcroft Lane in Mobberley. His love of mountaineering came from school trips to the Alps. He studied at history at Cambridge, but his love of mountains took him to Roquebrune-Cap-Martin in the Alpes-Maritimes to improve his French. When war came he was commissioned in the Royal Garrison Artillery as second lieutenant in December 1915 and assigned to the 40th Siege Battery, where he participated in the shelling of the Somme. He served as a liaison officer with the French and was promoted to first lieutenant before being invalided home.

The 1921 Mount Everest reconnaissance expedition team members. Standing (left to right): Wollaston, Howard-Bury, Heron and Raeburn. Sitting (left to right): Mallory, Wheeler, Bullock and Morshead. This was taken at the 17,300-ft advanced base camp.

School teaching did not suit him, and he was persuaded to join the first Everest expedition in 1921 because it would make his name and enhance his career as an educator or writer. In 1921, he explored the Tibetan side of Everest and reached the North Col with Guy Henry Bullock of the diplomatic service, who was a school friend

Stained-glass window at St Wilfred's Church, Mobberley.

of Mallory's at Winchester, and several porters. Earlier they had glimpsed a valley on the Nepali side of Everest that Mallory named the Western Cwm.

In 1922, he returned to Everest and reached 8,200 metres without supplemental oxygen, saving the lives of three companions when they slipped on the descent. After George Finch's party went even higher with oxygen, Mallory led an ill-advised attempt to reach the North Col after a heavy snowstorm that resulted in the deaths of seven porters in an avalanche.

Mallory lectured on Everest in Britain in 1922 and in America in 1923. The *New York Times* reported on 18 March 1923 that when asked why climb Everest, Mallory replied, 'Because it's there.'

In 1924, Mallory was promoted to climbing leader on Everest when Colonel E. F. Norton unexpectedly replaced General C. G. Bruce, who had fallen ill, as overall leader. Despite a prevailing prejudice, which he had shared, against oxygen, Mallory wanted to use it after seeing the benefits in 1922 and as he became increasingly obsessed with conquering the mountain. He developed a plan to give himself the best shot at the top by using oxygen with Andrew Irvine. He told his wife: 'It is almost unthinkable with this plan that I shan't get to the top: I can't see myself coming down defeated.'

After two unsuccessful attempts without oxygen, he put his plan into action. Mallory and Irvine left their camp on the north-east ridge on 8 June 1924 and were seen momentarily through a break in the clouds by Noel Odell, who said they were probably on a rock outcrop known as the Second Step, below the final summit pyramid. Their location during this sighting has been the subject of debate. After they failed to return, a memorial cairn was erected at the foot of Everest. That may well have been the end of this historic story, that is until Mallory's body was found in 1999.

An expedition dedicated to searching for Mallory and Irvine found Mallory's frozen body on a snow terrace at 27,000 feet. The body was identified by a name tag sewn into Mallory's clothing. After a brief ceremony, Mallory's body was reburied in the snow on 1 May 1999.

The mystery of whether they reached the top is unanswered. The camera that might tell us is still not found.

May Day

May Day has been celebrated since ancient times as a welcome to spring and summer. When we see the fair arriving and the maypole going up on the heath we know May Day is near. There are celebrations all over the country, but Knutsford has always celebrated in style. Not only do we have a wonderful procession, dancing on the heath and, of course, the fair, but May Day brings families together. The town is busy with family reunions – Knutsfordians all come back for May Day. They all turn out come rain or shine. The bells of Saint John's ring out in celebration. Maypoles have long been a tradition, but in the Puritan era they were banned as in 1644 Cromwell ordered them to be removed. Thankfully, the restoration brought back the king and also maypoles.

On Monday 2 May 1864, Annie Sarah Pollitt was the first May queen and Thomas Mullin was the crown bearer. The ceremony began at 2.30 when the band of the 15th Cheshire Rifle Volunteers marched to Cross Town schools and the children joined the procession.

The date 2 May 1887 was a very big day for Knutsford when the Prince and Princess of Wales visited the town for May Day. The royal family were hosted by Lord Egerton at Tatton Hall. What a day it must have been for May Howarth, the first royal May queen.

In 1890, the Jack in the Green entered the procession, a tradition carried to this day. It is often thought to be a fertility symbol. A unique feature is the sanding of the streets for May Day. This custom started as celebration for weddings; indeed, Mrs Gaskell stated, 'when I married at Knutsford Parish Church nearly all the houses were sanded.'

May Day was cancelled during the First World War and Ida Rose Jackson was the queen in 1919 when the town celebrated the end of the war. Celebrations were cancelled once more from 1939 until 1947 for the Second World War. It has taken the pandemic of 2020 to have May Day cancelled again.

May Day decorations on Princess Street, *c.* 1910.

May Day crowning.

Maypole dancers.

Norbury Booths Hall

This was the home of the Legh family for more than 600 years. Norbury means 'north fortified place' and there are still Norbury families in Knutsford to this day. John de Legh bought the site from William de Tabley in 1296. He first built his home on a moated site to the east of the present hall. The house was moated for security and also to impress the neighbours. The hall is believed to have looked very much like Little Moreton Hall, an impressive half-timbered building we can still see today.

The de Leghs were a notable family in Cheshire and John de Legh's grandson fought with the Black Prince at Poitiers in 1356. Another John de Legh became sherriff of Cheshire. The family continued to prosper and bought further land in Knutsford, Sudlow and Tabley. During the Civil War the family supported Parliament, but unfortunately the Parliamentary troops mutinied as they had not been paid. They imprisoned John de Legh in Chester until the troops were reimbursed.

Peter Legh built his new hall in 1745. It is built in the Palladian style using local brick and stone settings. The architect was believed to be John Garlive, who designed the parish church. The impressive staircase in the entrance hall can still be seen, although the hall is much altered now. The Legh family crest holds an erect sword and a snake around it. We still have the Legh arms, but it was formerly known as the Sword and Serpent.

Norbury Booths Hall, 1745.

Nuclear Knutsford

In 1954, the United Kingdom Atomic Energy Authority was established to oversee and pioneer the development of nuclear energy within the United Kingdom. This was the start of Knutsford's role in the history of nuclear power. In 1955, Booths Hall was leased to C. A. Parsons to become the headquarters of the Nuclear Power Plant Company. Eminent scientists were now arriving in Knutsford from all over the country. They first arrived on 1 June 1955 and started to work on the design of Bradwell Power Station. By September 1956 there were 156 staff at the hall.

The design, procurement, construction and commissioning of nuclear power stations employed skilled engineers, chemists, draughtsmen and technicians. At its peak National Nuclear Corporation at Booths Hall employed 1,700 staff. Radbrook Hall was also a centre for nuclear research. The hall was sold by the Hardy family in 1956 to the Nuclear Power Group who built offices and a testing tower on the grounds.

Above:
Booths Hall
staff.

Right:
Booths Hall
staff.

Obelisk

The obelisk on Chelford Road still stands and can be seen from the front of the hall.

Joan Leach tells us that 'it was a fashionable feature designed to be seen from Booths Hall and marked on the 1872 map as a monument to Ralph Leycester and his wife'. It has also been suggested that it is connected to the Leycester family of Toft. It was demolished by a car accident and there were holes that you could see both Toft and Booths Hall through. The obelisk is topped by a stone urn, probably from the old chapel.

Booth Obelisk, Knutsford.

Obelisk.

P

Paratroopers

Tatton Park was a crucial training ground for Britain's airborne forces in the Second World War. In June 1940, Prime Minister Winston Churchill issued one of his incisive memoranda, instructing that a force of 5,000 trained Allied paratroopers be created forthwith. It was decided to establish a Central Landing School (CLS – later to be known as the Parachute Training School, or PTS) at Manchester's Ringway Airport. The choice of location was driven by the need to be far enough away from German raids and the intense fighter and bomber activity over the eastern counties. It was quickly realised that Ringway would be too busy to act as a landing ground for the trainee paratroopers and alternative locations were considered.

Squadron Leader Louis Strange, commanding officer, had been a well-known pilot even before his First World War exploits and had met Lord Egerton, who was also an early aviator. Knowing of Maurice Egerton's large, secluded estate, strategically located just 5 miles south of Ringway, Strange therefore visited Tatton Park on 6 July, securing his lordship's ready agreement to use the park, initially only as the main dropping zone. Strange recorded:

> [Maurice] gave us every possible support, assistance and encouragement. We cut down his trees, we knocked down his gateposts, and we landed all over his park. I cannot ever remember him having any complaints, he was always helpful and full of encouragement. He would suggest that such and such a tree ought to come down.

Over the next four years British Army parachutists trained by the PTS at Ringway and Tatton Park were joined by Marine Commandos and RAF personnel. Many overseas troops were also trained, including American, Belgian, Canadian, Czech, Dutch, Norwegian and Polish. The first night drops of trainees by the PTS were made in moonlight on 14 January 1941. By 13 March, 3,890 live drops had been made from the Whitleys involving four fatalities and twenty-five broken limbs.

A mysterious 'Mr Y' made a 'special instructional descent' on Tatton Park at 6.30 a.m. on 1 September. We may assume that this was the first of several thousand men and around 100 women special agents from the Special Operations Executive who learned to

Above: Paratroopers training in Tatton.

Left: Parachute memorial.

parachute here. Their training was also segregated to maintain secrecy and anonymity. The agent's course was kept to five days with four live jumps. Odette Churchill, Violette Szabo, Evelyn Waugh and agents from many countries trained here. Some made special requests, such as to be dropped in Lord Egerton's trees in order to simulate their planned clandestine arrival in wooded country in occupied Europe. Their missions were extremely risky and many were captured and shot as spies, including Violette.

A section of free French personnel arrived at Ringway on 13 February 1941 and were inspected by General de Gaulle on 3 March. Winston Churchill, initiator of the Allied Airborne Forces, came to inspect progress personally on 26 April 1941, accompanied by Mrs Churchill, US Ambassador Averill Harriman, General Ismay and Air Marshall Sir Arthur Barratt.

A memorial in the grounds of Tatton Park commemorates No. 1 Parachute Training School, based at Ringway Airport, now Manchester Airport, during the Second World War. Tatton Park was used as a drop zone. The inscription reads:

> Throughout most of the second world war Tatton Park was the dropping zone for no.1 parachute training school, Ringway. this stone is set in honour of those thousands from many lands who descended here in the course of training, given or received, for parachute service with the allied forces in every theatre of war.

Penny-farthing

Penny-farthings and their brave riders are well known in Knutsford as they always accompany the May Day parade. Riding them takes great practice and a fearless personality. The town has hosted the 1 km Knutsford Great Race on the moor every ten years since 1980. The 1980 race had fifteen team entries and there were sixteen in 1990 and 2000. The 2010 race was limited to fifty teams. Riders come from around the world. The race challenges riders to a 3-hour endurance test. The race due in September 2020 was sadly cancelled due to the coronavirus pandemic. The penny-farthing was the first bicycle and it was also known as a 'high wheeler'. It was popular in the 1870s and 1880s, with its large front wheel providing high speeds (owing to it travelling a large distance for every rotation of the legs) and comfort (the large wheel provides greater shock absorption).

The name came from the British penny and farthing coins, the former being much larger than the latter, so that the side view resembles a larger penny and a smaller farthing.

It was invented in 1871 by British engineer James Starley. The penny-farthing came after the development of the hobby horse and the French velocipede, or 'Boneshaker' –

Penny Farthing Museum.

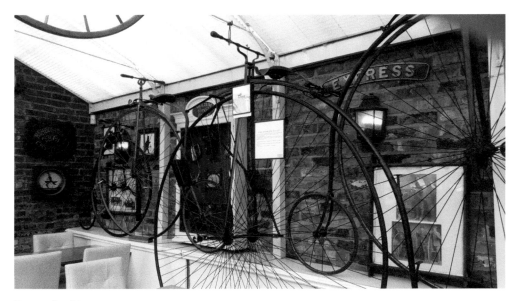

Penny-farthing.

all versions of early bikes. However, the penny-farthing was the first really efficient bicycle, consisting of a small rear wheel and large front wheel pivoting on a simple tubular frame with tires of rubber.

It became obsolete from the late 1880s with the development of modern bicycles, which provided similar speed amplification via chain-driven gear trains and comfort through pneumatic tyres. They were marketed in comparison to penny-farthings as 'safety bicycles' because of the reduced danger of falling and the reduced height to fall from.

Do visit the Courtyard Coffee House on the bottom street and enjoy the Penny Farthing Museum, where you can be taken back through history to the pride of the Victorian era.

The museum has some of the oldest penny-farthings in the country as well as some of the smallest and largest too. There's plenty to admire with your tea and home-made cake in the café.

Penny

Edward Penny RA was born in Silk Mill Street in 1714. The Freemasons Arms bears a blue plaque to acknowledge his birthplace. Many in his family had pursued a career in the Church or as a surgeon, such as his twin brother Henry Penny; however, Edward pursued his interest in painting and was sent to London to study with Thomas Hudson, whose influence is clearly evident in his early portraits. He subsequently studied in Rome with the portrait painter Marco Benefial. In around 1748 he returned to England and began to execute portraits in all formats. Just as his contemporary

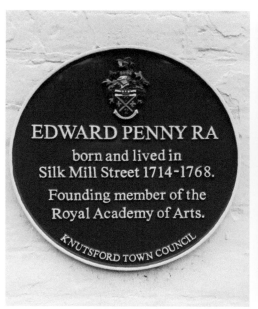

Above left: Edward Penny's plaque, Silkmill Street.

Above right: Edward Penny, RA.

Sir Joshua Reynolds imbued portraiture with the grand manner, Penny developed a highly original amalgam of history painting and genre, infusing historical events with the quotidian and genre scenes with the gravitas of more elevated subjects. The first works he exhibited at the Society of Artists in 1762 were a small whole length of a lady and a scene from Nicholas Rowe's *Jane Shore*. Penny became the vice president of the Society of Artists in 1765, a position he held until his resignation from the society in 1768. He then became one of the founders of the Royal Academy and was appointed the first professor of painting. Penny resigned his professorship of painting on 31 December 1781 due to ill health. In May 2018, Andrew Penny, a descendant of Edward Penny, visited Knutsford to open a major exhibition at Knutsford Heritage Centre, telling the story of the artist's life. His paintings are still sought after. Many of his portraits are still selling well at auctions today.

Princess Street (Top Street)

Princess Street was developed in the early 1900s as a residential street running parallel with the original King Street. The area between the two streets was a mass of steps. Several imposing Georgian houses were built. Slowly, many of the houses opened shops at street level. The houses had large gardens that stretched right across St Edward Road, which was built to relieve the traffic in Princess Street. In the centre was The George Tap. This was to cater for the many coachmen, ostlers and grooms who served the coaching trade at the George Hotel. The prices were low and many locals would take a jug to be filled with ale to take home. Opposite was the fictional home of Miss Matty in *Cranford*. On the left we come to the Methodist Church.

Red Cow Hotel, Princess Street.

Princess Street.

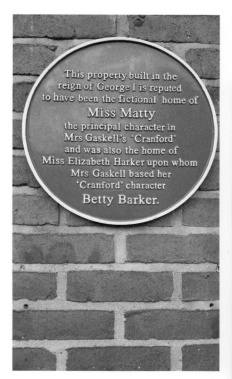

Above: Miss Matty's plaque, Princess Street.

Right: Knutsford Methodist Church with Wesley's step.

In March 1738, Revd John Wesley preached for the first time in the town from the steps of a house near the George Hotel. The present church was opened in 1865 and was designed by T. R. Clements and described by Pevsner as 'Gothic with a wild tower which has lost its spire'.

There had been an established history of over 120 years of Methodist-style worship in the town. The very same steps from which it is believed that Wesley preached are now preserved (presented to the chapel in 1932) in front of the current church building. Nearby is Lloyds Bank, which was built as the Savings Bank and has a fine Grecian ashlar façade by Robert Gregson.

We have the Egertons to thank for the Old Town Hall. They funded this grand building in 1870. They appointed Alfred Waterhouse as the architect. The ground floor was open and provided a market area for local traders. It was never really suitable as a council chamber. It was used by the WVS during the war and later as a centre for the Knutsford Boys' Club. It has been well restored and is now the Lost and Found.

Left: The Savings
Bank.

Below: Old Town
Hall, Toft Road.

Lost and Found.

Quarter Sessions

Knutsford's prestige was enhanced in 1575 when the quarterly sessions were held in the town above the market hall. Juries of up to fifteen men were appointed from the freeholders. At this time, quarter sessions were held in rotation between Knutsford, Chester, Nantwich, Northwich and Middlewich. A Sessions House was built in 1760 in Canute Place, where the bank stands on the corner of Princess Street. Knutsford then became more significant as it only shared the justice of the county with Chester. In 1816, the magistrates met at The George to consider a new Sessions House and house of correction. The choice of Knutsford again was a great boost the town's economy.

George Moneypenny was appointed architect, winning the competition with his design built in ashlar stone with a grand Grecian portico. There were problems, however. The building costs kept mounting as the price of transporting the stone was underestimated. There was a special four-storey wing to hold 100 women. The gaol was not without controversy. In 1843, a select committee looked into the discipline and management at the gaol. Chartist prisoners complained that on arrival they were addressed in an aggressive and violent manner by the gaoler. They were made to walk the treadmill for the amusement of visitors. There was also an accusation that the overseer himself was himself a felon. They also, perhaps not surprisingly, complained about the quantity and quality of the food. The typical daily ration was bread and gruel for breakfast, 1 quart of pea soup for dinner, and bread and gruel for supper. The governor did not lose his job.

It is gruesome to think that executions took place here. The first was of Owen McGill, who was found guilty of murdering his wife. The church bell toiled when he was hanged at 8.00 a.m. The huge gaol at the rear, which could accommodate over 800 prisoners, was demolished in the 1930s. It had ceased serving as a county gaol before the First World War and during the war it housed prisoners of war. In 1846, a fine house was built for the governor of the gaol, designed by Edmund Sharpe in a Georgian style. It is constructed in brick with a slate roof and is in two storeys. It was later used as council offices and is now used for Knutsford Town Council.

The Sessions House, with its solid classical structure and Ionic portico, still dominates Toft Road. In 1952, the trial of Alan Turing was held here. He was being prosecuted for 'homosexual acts' and was ultimately found guilty of 'gross indecency'. It was a terrible episode in the life of this war hero. Turing had played a crucial role in cracking intercepted coded messages that enabled the Allies to defeat the Nazis. He tragically died by suicide in 1954 – just two years after his conviction. In 2013, Turing was given a posthumous pardon by the Queen, and in 2017 the law commonly termed the 'Alan Turing law' was passed to retroactively pardon men charged with historical homosexual convictions.

The last trial at the courthouse was in May 2010.

Sessions House and prison.

Governor's House.

Racecourse

Who would have thought that in the eighteenth century Knutsford Races was as famous as Chester Races? Although, Chester is the oldest racecourse, having started in 1539.

Knutsford races were established in 1729. The 1791 guide to Cheshire noted 'The annual race meeting at Knutsford is remarkable for being honoured with a more brilliant assemblage of nobility and gentry than any other in the country; not excepting Chester.'

Horse racing on Knutsford Heath had been somewhat of an attraction for more than 200 years. Back then the gentry – mainly from Cheshire country houses – raced their horses and gambled at the cockpit. The races were in summertime and this gave the grand houses around Knutsford encouragement to host large garden parties. An 1815 print entitled *The Adventures of Knutsford Racecourse* shows a large grandstand, stalls and booths. In 1865, a more elegant grandstand was opened by the Knutsford Grandstand Company. They were hoping to attract customers arriving on the railway

The racecourse, 1815.

that had recently arrived in the town. Races were advertised and special trains ran. Unfortunately, the arrival of the newcomers meant that the old supporters – the Cheshire gentry – lost interest. Racing ended in 1873 when Lord Egerton refused permission to use the heath. This list of early Knutsford gold cup winners shows how the races were dominated by the local gentry:

1815: Prince of Orange, owned by Lord Grey.
1816: Little Thomas, owned by Mr Painter.
1817: Orontes, owned by Lord Grosvenor.
1818: Tagus, owned by Lord Grosvenor
1819: Advance, owned by Mr Clifton.
1820: Astbury, owned by Sir J. Egerton.
1821: Tarragon, owned by Sir T. Stanley.

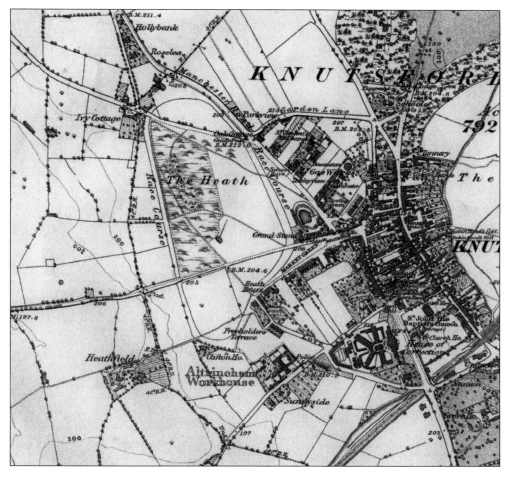

Racecourse map, 1872.

1822: Tarragon, owned by Sir T. Stanley.
1823: Princess Royal, owned by Sir T. Mostyn.
1824: General Mina, owned by Sir T. Stanley.
1825: Hajji Baba, owned by Sir T. Stanley.
1826: Mr Munn, owned by Mr Clifton.
1827: Signorina, owned by Sir W. Wynn.
1828: Longwaist, owned by Mr Nowell.
1829: Halston, owned by Mr Mytton.
1830: Guido, owned by Mr Clifton.
1831: Birmingham, owned by Mr Beardsworth.
1832: Liverpool, owned by Lord Cleveland.
1833: Lady Stafford, owned by Mr Bower.

Royce, Henry

Henry Royce started life as a newspaper boy, but he was already showing a great interest in engineering by this time. After working in various firms he set up H. Royce & Co., manufacturers of components such as doorbells and dynamos in Cooke Street, Manchester. The company flourished and Royce set up home in Knutsford. Rolls-Royce was conceived in Manchester when Charles Stewart Rolls met Henry Royce in The Midland Hotel, Peter Street, Manchester. The meeting was arranged by Henry Edmunds, a member of the Automobile Club Committee. Like all great stories, there is some doubt surrounding it: Henry Edmunds called it the Great Central Hotel rather

Brae Cottage.

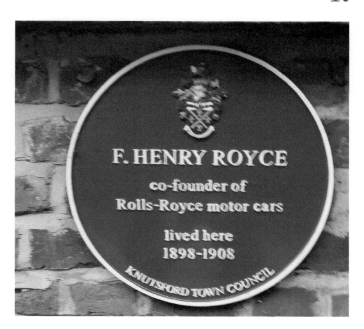

Henry Royce's plaque.

than The Midland; however, there is no doubt that the meeting was in the great city of Manchester.

This meeting would change the future of motoring forever. The minute Rolls set eyes on the twin-cylinder 10 hp he knew he had found what he was looking for. He took it for a ride and agreed to sell as many motor cars as Royce could build, under the name Rolls-Royce. A future model was advertised as 'the six-cylinder Rolls-Royce – not one of the best, but the best car in the World.'

The Royces moved to a newly built house in Knutsford in 1898. You can still see Brae Cottage in Legh Road today. He was the first person in the Knutsford to light his house with electricity. He was a proud gardener and a dedicated rose and fruit tree grower. Cars, however, were his passion and by the end of 1903 he had designed and built his first petrol engine. In April 1904, all eyes were on him when he drove his first Royce 10-hp motor car from his factory in Cooke Street, Manchester, to Knutsford.

Silk

Most histories of the silk industry in England begin with the arrival of French refugees to Spitalfields in London; however, silk was prepared for embroidery in Macclesfield by the Middle Ages and the silk button trade was soon well-established. The craft then spread to towns like Knutsford.

A silk mill was established in 1753 and gave its name to Silk Mill Street, which runs between King Street and Princess Street. The mill was founded by Pool Hurst and John Skellorn. Silk buttons were a favourite in the fashions of the time. The row of weavers'

Silk mill.

cottages at the north end of King Street indicates the presence of small-scale weaving. The site of the new parish church on Church Hill was known as Tenters' Field. This well-drained, sloping site was ideal for the bleaching of linen cloth, which was stretched on tenterhooks. The well-known phrase 'on tenterhooks', meaning a state of tension, came from this process. The silk mill was converted into three dwellings in 1818 and then into a public house in the 1890s. The textile trade did not last long in the town, but the names remain not only Silk Mill Street but also Cotton Shop Yard.

Smith, William

William Smith was a trumpeter at the Charge of the Light Brigade. In 1854, during the Crimean War, the British light cavalry led by Lord Cardigan fought the Battle of Balaclava. The assault went badly wrong when there was miscommunication in the chain of command, and the Light Brigade was sent on a frontal assault against a well-prepared artillery battery with excellent fields of defensive fire. The Light Brigade reached the battery under withering direct fire and scattered some of the gunners, but they were forced to retreat immediately and the assault ended with very high British casualties and no decisive gains. These tragic events were the subject of Alfred, Lord Tennyson's narrative poem 'The Charge of the Light Brigade' (1854), published just six weeks after the event. Its lines emphasise the valour of the cavalry in bravely carrying out their orders, regardless of the nearly inevitable outcome.

A Knutsford man rode into the valley of death. He rode... and lived to tell the tale. William Smith was promoted to trumpet-major immediately after the Charge of the

Above left: William Smith.

Above right: Plaque on Stanley Road.

Light Brigade, and even wrote a poem about his experiences, 'Balaclava Heights', although it never rivalled Lord Tennyson's famous work in popularity. After his discharge, Smith and his wife Mary Jane lived at Freehold Terrace, Love Lane (now Stanley Road), and in 1863 he became trumpet-major to the Earl of Chester's Cheshire Yeomanry. He retired in 1874, became crier at the quarter sessions held at Chester and Knutsford, and was manager of Knutsford Gentlemen's Club. He was a well-known local character who regularly sang at recitals, functions and entertainments.

In early November 1879 he went on a brandy-drinking spree, which seemed to make him depressed. He was often troubled with colds, and on 15 November he told a number of people that they would never see him again before sending a friend to the chemist to buy laudanum, a strong opium-based sedative, which he said was to make a cough mixture. He withdrew £15 from the bank to settle his debts in the town, drank the potion and died, aged fifty-seven. An inquest at the White Bear Hotel in Knutsford found that he had died of 'apoplexy, probably accelerated by laudanum, taken while he was in an unsound state of mind'.

He was buried at Knutsford Parish Church. In 1951, a plaque was placed on his former home in Stanley Road. It reads: 'Trumpet-Major William Smith, 1822–1879, who sounded the charge at Balaclava, lived here.'

Stringer Family

Thomas Stringer worked as a servant at Norbury Booths Hall, although as a young man he showed much natural talent as an animal painter. Stringer's relationship with Peter Legh, however, was difficult and after an argument Stringer left his employer to become a full-time artist.

His talent in painting horses was quickly recognised by the local gentry, who commissioned him to paint their dogs and horses. His painting *Thomas Egerton's*

Turpin by Thomas Stringer. (Courtesy of Mike Peel under Creative Commons 1.0)

The Kilton.

Chestnut Hunter with a Groom and Two Hounds and a Terrier in a River Landscape sold at Sotheby's for £46,259 in 2014.

He did so well that he was able to send his two sons, Samuel and Daniel, to the Royal Academy to study under another Knutsford artist, Professor Edward Penny. Thomas and Samuel (his eldest son) painted many of the local pub signs, such as The Smoker at Plumley, The Kilton and The Slow and Easy at Lostock – all racehorses owned by the local landowners.

Daniel went to London in 1770, aged sixteen. His progress was outstanding. Penny declared that Daniel was the best draughtsmen who ever entered the academy. All three men were gifted, but it was Daniel who was the most talented. Many considered his talent to be equal to Gainsborough or Sir Joshua Reynolds. He painted several large studies for the Liverpool Royal Exchange – sadly all lost when the building was burnt to the ground. His *Portrait of the Artist* (1776) is owned by the Tate Gallery. A more unusual project was his design for a Wedgewood dinner service for Catherine, the Empress of Russia, which can still be seen in the Hermitage Museum at St Petersburg. Daniel married Ann Boulton at St John's, Knutsford, in 1786. His brother Samuel had died two year earlier, so Daniel Leech was his best man. The marriage does not seem to have been a happy one. Sadly, he became lethargic and lost his enthusiasm for his art. He became fond of low company and was often drunk. This was a sad end to a very talented career. Here is a quote from his contemporary at the academy: 'I called on him at his house in Knutsford. All his skill and love of art had, I found, been sacrificed to his delight in Cheshire ale.'

In 1986 a self-portrait by Daniel was bought by Manchester City Art Gallery for £1,210.

Tatton

The Tatton Estate was bought by Sir Thomas Egerton, Lord Chancellor of England in 1598.

His son John Egerton succeeded to his titles and to the Tatton Estate and was created Earl of Bridgewater in 1617. There was once an ancient village of Tatton and it was here that the original medieval hall was built. The atmospheric great hall was grandly decorated with carved ferns, artichokes and rosettes. Sir Thomas added to this manor house with additional servants' quarters and bedchambers. In 1770, the hall was deemed to be too humble for the family and plans were made to build a much larger, grander hall in the neoclassical style. When the new hall was built, the old hall became a farmhouse. The new hall was designed by the Wyatt family and it was considered a great success. The main body of the hall and the family wing to

Tatton Hall.

The south side of Tatton Hall.

the west, both in two storeys, are built in ashlar Runcorn sandstone with slate and lead roofs. The additions of 1884 (the family entrance hall and smoking room) are faced in yellow terracotta. The south front of the hall has seven bays. At its centre is a large Corinthian portico with four monolithic columns. The north front is simpler in design, also with seven bays, and it has a pedimented porch with two columns. The east front has five bays with Corinthian pilasters on a slightly projecting plinth and an entablature above. The family wing has seven bays. The south front has a Tuscan colonnade on the lower storey and an Ionic colonnade, veranda and balustrade above. The orangery is a conservatory designed by Lewis Wyatt. It is built in sandstone on a stone plinth and has a glass roof. The orangery has a cross-plan and a front of seven bays, the outer bays being angled. The grounds and parkland were also laid out at this time. The Knutsford gates, built in ashlar stone, consist of a triple gateway and a lodge on the west side. Each gateway contains a cast-iron gate. The central gateway is flanked by Doric columns.

Wilbraham Egerton was passionate about his gardens and he added a botanical garden and was responsible for inviting the Princess of Wales to visit Tatton in 1887, and they even visited the May Day festivities. Other eminent guests included the Shah of Persia and the Crown Prince of Siam.

In 1910, Alan de Tatton Egerton added the wonderful Japanese garden after having invited Japanese gardeners to construct it.

Knutsford Gate.

Toft Hall

Originally the hall was owned by a family called Toft in the reign of Richard the Lionheart. It came to be in the hands of the Leycester family through the marriage with Joan Toft. The fine hall we see today was rebuilt in the late seventeenth century. It was stuccoed in the early nineteenth century to give the hall its distinctive design. Built in two storeys with distinctive four-storey towers, it is a designated Grade II listed building.

The Leycester family were always involved with local affairs. In 1841, a school was built on Toft Road. It was also used as a meeting hall and food was distributed from here in the war years. In 1854, Toft also had its own church. It was built as a memorial for her husband Sir Ralph Gerard Leycester, who had died in 1851 at the early age of thirty-five. The site was chosen to be in good view of the hall. The idea of their very own church was inspired by the news that Peter Legh was building a new church at Cross Town. When the Leycester family left the hall it served as a health hydro and was a prisoner-of-war camp during the war before becoming offices for several companies.

Toft Hall.

Toft School.

Toft Church.

U

Unitarian Chapel, Brook Street

The origins of Unitarianism came from the religious intolerance at the end of the seventeenth century. The Act of Uniformity (1662) required all clergymen to give their 'unfeigned assent and consent' to the Book of Common Prayer. At first, services were held in secret in supporters' homes. In 1689, in the reign of William and Mary, the Toleration Act allowed dissenters to build their own chapels. Dissenters had always been strong in Knutsford. The land at the bottom of Adams Hill was given by Isaac Antrobus and in 1689 the chapel was opened. It was originally known as New Meeting House, as Knutsford was then in the parish of Rostherne. This fine chapel is the oldest religious building in the town. It is built in red brick with a stone-flagged roof in two storeys with two external staircases. Inside is a gallery on three sides and a pulpit on a long wall. The chapel will always be associated with Mrs Gaskell; indeed, she was a Sunday school teacher here. She described it vividly in her novel *Ruth*. She is buried

Unitarian Chapel, Brook Street.

Brook Street
calendar 1906.

here with her husband William. Revd George Payne was minister of Brook Street Chapel from 1890 to 1930. He founded Knutsford Literary Society and was honorary secretary of Knutsford Library He wrote *Knutsford and Mrs Gaskell* and a history of the chapel.

Uttley

Alison Uttley, the author of the charming Little Grey Rabbit books, lived at the Old Vicarage on the corner of King Street and Drury Lane. She was born the daughter of a tenant hill farmer at Castle Top Farm in Matlock, Derbyshire. It was the memories of her childhood here that gave her a great love of the countryside, nature and old country ways. Many of the characters in her books are based on the people she grew up with in the Derbyshire peaks. She created the enduringly charming children's characters Little Grey Rabbit and Fuzzypeg the Hedgehog. All her animals are very human and yet very wise. She wrote over fourteen children's books and twenty-two adult books, including the reminiscent *The Family on the Hill* and *The Country Child*.

Alison gained a degree in physics from Manchester University and then trained to be a teacher. It was her marriage to James Uttley that brought her to live in Knutsford.

The old vicarage.

His family lived in south Manchester. It was not a happy marriage. He was prone to depression and drowned himself in the River Mersey in 1930.

In later life Alison said that she began writing to support herself and her son financially after she was widowed, but in fact her first book, *The Squirrel, the Hare and the Little Grey Rabbit*, was published in 1929, before her husband's death. They later moved to No. 13 Higher Downs, Bowdon, which now has a blue plaque. Her difficult personal life, the death of her husband and having to bring her beloved son up alone possibly resulted in a rather embittered personality. She quarrelled fiercely with her own illustrator, Margaret Tempest. She moved south to Beaconsfield in 1938. Enid Blyton was a neighbour and there must have been a lot of jealousy between them as she described Enid as a 'boastful and vulgar woman'. She also did not have kind words for Beatrix Potter and hated to be compared with her. She suffered ill health in later life, but she was delighted when she received an honorary doctorate degree by the University of Manchester in 1970. She gave great joy to children and her characters are beloved to this day. She died in 1976 and just a simple bunch of wildflowers were placed on her coffin. Her only son, John, born in 1914, also died by suicide just two years after his mother's death, by driving off a cliff in 1978. She gave great joy to children and her characters are beloved to this day. When she died in 1976 a simple bunch of wildflowers were placed on her coffin.

Left: The Uttley plaque, Drury Lane.

Below: The Old Vicarage.

V

Vikings

King Cnut (Canute) is recognised as one of the most prominent kings of the Anglo-Saxon era. He conquered England, Denmark, Norway and areas of Sweden. Cnut was a Viking and is probably best known as such today. He led his army using Viking tactics and launched raids on enemy territory using instantly recognisable longships. He first arrived in England with his father, Sweyn Forkbeard, and opposed King Æthelred 'the Unready'. Sweyn was not just raiding England; by this time he was trying to conquer it. It soon looked like Sweyn was about to become king of the

King Canute sculpture on Toft Road, designed by Christine Wilcox-Baker and donated to the town council in 2014.

country; he had been so successful in battle that King Æthelred had fled. But then, just as it appeared that Sweyn's triumph was complete, he suddenly died.

Another opportunity arose for Cnut in 1016. Following the death of the Anglo-Saxon King Æthelred his son Edmund Ironside became king of England. However, Ironside did not have unanimous support, even from the English. Some seem to have reasoned that Cnut, who had returned to the country with a newly raised army, was a better bet. Cnut and Edmund fought a vicious and drawn-out war. After several major clashes, the conflict's final climactic battle was fought at Ashingdon in Essex. Cnut was now the undisputed successor to the English throne, and he was crowned at the old Saint Paul's Cathedral in January 1017.

In 1027, Cnut travelled to Scotland where the Scottish kings acknowledged Cnut as the legitimate ruler of England, bringing peace to the two countries. This would indeed have brought him through Cheshire. While he may not have forded the River Lily, he may well have forded the mere and marshes nearby. Cnut was buried in Winchester, which was the capital of the kingdom of Wessex, and his remains are now held in Winchester Cathedral.

Volunteers

The French Revolution was causing concern at home when William Pitt called for the setting up of county volunteers. The regiment was founded in 1797 when Sir John Leicester of Tabley raised a county regiment of light cavalry in response to the growing fears of invasion from Napoleonic France. In 1798, the Knutsford Volunteers were formed with Sir John Leicester, as Colonel George Leycester of Toft

Cheshire Regiment memorial, Chester Cathedral. (Courtesy of Andrew Rabbott under Creative Commons 3.0)

led the Knutsford Royal Volunteer Infantry. Their armoury was the Market House, off King Street, and when the building was demolished for flats in the 1970s their pikes were still hanging on the wall. They did not see military action, but they were called out to deal with civil unrest. It is not to their credit that they were at the Peterloo Massacre when the yeomanry charged the innocent crowd. Sir John Leicester was not present, complaining that the mishandling of the yeomanry made them obnoxious to their neighbours. They made a more glorious part in George III's Golden Jubilee celebrations. The Cheshire Regiment served bravely through the Boer War and both world wars. Sadly in 1999 the Cheshire Yeomanry was amalgamated into the Royal Mercian and Lancastrian Yeomanry.

(St) Vincent's

By 1861 the number of Catholics in Knutsford had increased and there were calls for a Catholic church. Funding, however, was not available. A priest would visit from Altrincham and rooms were made available on Manchester Road. Eventually a small church was built on Queen Street. Later a priest's house and a school were added. The priest had a difficult congregation as many were Irish labourers, and he often had to help them out after a night in the local pubs. This church is now the home of the Little Theatre.

A new church was built at the bottom of Queen Street in 1927 after many years of fundraising. Sadly, subsidence resulted in it becoming unsafe and in 1983 a third church for Catholics to worship was dedicated. This church still stands today and a modern school was provided in Manor Park South.

Little Theatre, Queen Street.

Watson's

This was a Knutsford institution on the corner of Church Hill. William Watson opened his store in 1856. He was a local man, originally a cabinetmaker. He must have had a good eye for business when he decided to become a grocer. He sons followed him and the family business grew and grew. The shop employed forty-two in its heyday. Teas were blended, coffee beans ground, bacon cut to order and sugar and flour weighed. Watson's carts were everywhere, delivering around the town and to all the surrounding villages. Their freshly baked bread was renowned, the aroma filling the air along King Street. He extended his business up Church Hill. Watson's served Knutsford for 121 years, providing wonderful quality and service before finally closing in 1973.

Watson's, King Street.

W

Wives and Daughters

This was the last novel by Mrs Gaskell and was almost complete at the time of her death. It is another wonderful novel depicting houses and characters of Knutsford. The opening scenes are set in Lady Mary's school at the entrance to Tatton Park. It is now Knutsford Golf Club and it is said that Lady Mary still roams the building at times.

In a series of skilfully interwoven plots it tells the story of Molly Gibson, whose father, a doctor, has remarried. His new wife was Clare Kirkpatrick, a rather flighty widow. Clare's daughter, Cynthia, enters the story. She is as flighty as her mother and Molly come to her rescue as she helps her through the problems of her own making. Socially the book covers landowners, tenant farmers, labourers and servants. Giving once again a lively, informative picture of early nineteenth-century England.

In this book she named our town 'Hollingford' and Tatton Hall becomes 'Cumnor Towers'. Molly Gibson's house can still be seen on Toft Road today as Arthur Lee Interiors.

Lady Mary's school.

Xmas

Knutsford has always celebrated Christmas in style. The switching on of the Christmas lights has been a tradition for many years, with carol singing in Canute Place and a traditional nativity crèche.

Knutsford Christmas Market was launched in 2010 by volunteers Sarah Flannery and Kate Houghton. The inaugural Christmas market was a great success. 'It was wonderful to see the town buzzing, the tills ringing, charities benefiting and hordes of people enjoying all which this lovely town has to offer.'

Christmas Nativity.

Above: Christmas lights.

Right: Christmas market.

It was instigated to provide a footfall boost for Knutsford's town centre businesses and started off as a one-day market on Regent Street on the day of the Christmas lights switch on (Thursday, 2 December 2010). In 2011, it was expanded to run Friday and Saturday in two marquees on Silk Mill Street with sixty stalls in total. In 2013, the market was handed fully over to the town council. The lights switch on was moved to a Saturday and since then has been operated as a two-day (Saturday and Sunday) street market along Princess Street and Silk Mill Street with around 130 stalls per day. A highlight is the wonderful window displays in the local shops.

Christmas window display.

Y

Yankee Knutsford

In the period leading up to D-Day in 1944 Knutsford became to home to thousands of American soldiers. How they must have livened up the town? These young American GIs must have seemed very glamorous. The dances held at Over Peover village hall were a great success.

The heath was enclosed to provide a camp for the soldiers. Many of the officers were billeted in the town and there were 200–300 American soldiers living in huts at Peover Hall.

General Patton was stationed here in preparation for the D-Day landings and also to help to throw the Germans off the scent of what was really being planned. He was remembered in the village walking his Labrador around the lanes of Peover. He loved visiting the local pubs such as the Whipping Stocks and the Bells of Peover, where he once had lunch with Eisenhower. Patton used to worship at St Lawrence and he left

General Patton.

Bells of Peover.

he presented a flag – the Stars and Stripes – to the parish, which hangs in the church to this day.

General Patton had had a long and distinguished military career when he arrived in Knutsford. He was, however, always controversial, showing no sympathy for soldiers suffering battle fatigue. He was almost sacked after the infamous 'Knutsford Incident' outside the Old Town Hall. The building also authentically featured in a passage in the George C. Scott film of Patton from 1970. It all harked back to him delivering a controversial speech on the opening of a Welcome Club for American Servicemen just six weeks before D-Day. Patton made off-the-cuff remarks that it was the 'evident destiny' of America and Britain to rule the world one day. This was considered a slight to Russia, as they were mentioned only as an afterthought. This almost ended his career before his fame had begun. Eisenhower was furious, but Patton maintained the leak of the 'incident' was no accident but was in fact a set up by Churchill.

Zeitgeist – The Spirit or Essence of a Particular Time

Mrs Gaskell captured perfectly the spirit, manners and morals of a small town in the early nineteenth century in *Cranford*. She had already expressed life in Victorian England vividly in her first novel *Mary Barton: A Tale of Manchester Life*. She tells the story of the hungry 1940s, when poverty placed a heavy burden on the workers.

The cover from the Everyman edition, 1911.

There were other writers, notably Charles Dickens in *Hard Times*, who covered the hardship of the age, but *Mary Barton* expresses this time with empathy and compassion. Historians may outline life in a city like Manchester, but *Mary Barton* brings these hard times to life. The story covers riots and crimes that we are familiar with today. The hero, John Barton, is a good man, a weaver who in his struggle for justice is driven to commit murder. The Gaskells were heavily involved with the Lower Mosley Street schools. They were set up by the congregation of Cross Street Chapel to meet the needs of working-class children in basic education as well as in religious instruction. Both of them taught in the schools. What makes Mrs Gaskell exceptional is that when she arrived in Manchester and witnessed the hardships she not only wrote about it, she and her husband William worked tirelessly to help the poor and vulnerable.

Acknowledgments

Knutsford Heritage Centre
Audrey Young – Knutsford Historical Society
Knutsford Town Council and Jonathan Farber
Penny Farthing Museum

Bibliography

Green, Henry, *Knutsford Its Traditions and History* (E. J. Morten, 1859)
Leach, Joan, *Knutsford: A History* (Phillimore, 2007)
Payne, Revd George, *Mrs Gaskell and Knutsford* (1900)
Pevsner, *The Buildings of England: Cheshire* (1971)
The Oxford Literary Guide (Oxford University Press, 1977)

About the Authors

Jean spent her childhood in Knutsford and worked for Cheshire libraries for many years. She is now an adult tutor, offering courses in family history. John has numerous production credits in theatre, TV and film (BBC and Granada). He has worked for the last decade mainly in portrait, film and artscape photography. Jean and John made their home in Knutsford and have lived here for thirty years. Their previous publications include *Central Manchester Through Time*, *A–Z of Manchester*, *Historic England: Manchester*, *Runcorn at Work* and *Widnes at Work*.